Dear Sh[...]

Abundan[...]

of Love, [...]

heath, wholeness

& Light.

Love

Lauré ♡

Blessings
of
Gratitude

Blessings That Transform Your Life

Laurie Leah Levine

International Author of Spiritual Medicine

Blessings of Gratitude
Spiritual/Metaphyics/Self Help/Religion
Copyright © 2006 by Laurie Leah Levine

First Published 2006
By Touch For Life
PO Box 424
Pymble NSW Australia 2073

Disclaimer
This author does not dispense medical advice or prescribe the use of any technique as a replacement form of treatment for physical, mental or medical problems without the advice of your doctor, either directly or indirectly. The author's intention is to offer information and tools to help the reader in their quest for spiritual growth, emotional and physical wellbeing.

National Library of Australia Cataloguing-in-Publication entry:
Levine, Laurie.
Blessings of gratitude : blessings that transform your life.
ISBN 0-9775066-0-6
1. Gratitude - Religious aspects. 2. Spiritual healing.
3. Theology, Practical. I. Title.

203.1

Cover design by Roger Nelson
Inside design & layout by Sai Towers Publishing
Cover Artwork by Laurie Levine

This book is dedicated
to my beloved husband,
Stan Isaacman

Acknowledgment

I thank God for all the blessings in my life. I am so grateful for my beloved soul mate and husband Stan for loving me unconditionally. I give thanks to my parents, Sandy and Sylvia for their love and support, family members, friends, clients, Rev. Michael Beckwith; Agape International Spiritual Center & Emerson Institute, for all they have contributed to my life. I am thankful for my wonderful friends Ian, Robie, Susan, David, & Allan for their love, support and being angels in my life. I am grateful to all those involved with our Positive Living Spiritual Centre in Sydney. My blessings and thanks to Wendy-Ann Schober for her loving service and generous heart. To Beverly Lundell; my prayer partner, bless you for your consciousness, support and love. I give thanks to Jennifer Privateer and Nancy Shearer for editing my book.

Heartfelt thanks to Roger Nelson for designing my cover, and for his time, patience, friendship and support.

I am grateful to Sai Towers Publishing for the production of my book and to Sai Baba for his blessings of grace.

Testimonials

"Blessings from Laurie's book are a gift.   It is a gift for every aspect of living as we know it.   Dine from its blessings often and you will know the magic of a full heart, mind and spirit."

– Michael Beckwith, D.D.
Author of *40 Day Mind Fast Soul Feast*, Founder & Spiritual Director, Agape International Spiritual Center in Culver City, California

"Laurie's blessings transcend the ordinary.   All of us, at one time or another has experienced the emotions, relations, and feelings that Laurie has included in her blessings.   With Laurie's direction a personal negative may be turned into a powerful positive.   These blessings allow us to look within ourselves, giving us a choice as how to approach life."

– Ed Klein, M.D.
Author of *Soul Search: The Healing Possibilities Of Past Lives*

"I liken Laurie's book to Louise Hay's book, "You Can Heal Your Life." I love how Laurie has a blessing for any given situation that may come up in life. That way I can go directly to that blessing and begin the healing process for my 'issue.' This is a book that I will leave on my bedside table and use everyday! What a wonderful addition to my collection of books that inspires me."

– Nicolette Vajtay
Actress, Director & Playwright

"Bless a thing and it will bless you.   Curse it and it will curse you.   If you bless any situation, it has no power to hurt you, if you sincerely bless it."

– Emmet Fox

Contents

Blessings For Special Occasions And Ceremonies

Blessings For Major Holidays

Spiritual And Cultural Blessings

INTRODUCTION

I wrote this book because I have experienced how blessing and being grateful for everything I have in my life has helped get me through cancer, back injury, depression, divorce and many other changes. It has given me the strength and courage to move through difficult times with a positive attitude and helped me to overcome my fears. Through these blessings and focusing my mind on gratitude, I was able to accept what was happening easier and put my attention on what I have instead of what I thought I did not have. It has been a great source of support. I hope it does the same for you.

It can be a challenge sometimes to be able to feel grateful in the moment or to see something as a blessing when we are in pain or in emotional distress. It can take a little while sometimes to get to that place of recognition. Be gentle with yourself if this is what is happening for you.

The blessings in this book are written from a spiritual and metaphysical perspective. Some of the blessings may be a bit different from what you are used to. These blessings have been written to support you to see your experience in a new way and to connect you to the feeling of gratitude.

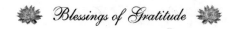

No matter what is happening, when you are able to feel grateful for your life, it helps to reduce fear and bring you back to feeling more peaceful again. I have found that no matter where we are in our spiritual development fears can still come up. It is what we do inside our mind that can make all the difference.

Think about a time that you experienced something good and unexpected coming out of a so-called "bad" situation.

Did you ever think about that experience as being a blessing?

I wanted to share with you something that happened to me. I found a nodule on my thyroid and when they operated to remove it they found it was cancerous. This experience has really shown me more than ever the power of gratitude and seeing every situation as a blessing. Whenever I felt fearful about the upcoming surgery or treatments I would need to undergo, I would bless my body, every aspect of my life and focus my attention on everything I am grateful for. I found this really helped me to stay in the present moment and significantly reduced the fear I was feeling. This experience has allowed me to teach from a much deeper place, to love myself and appreciate all that I have more than I have ever done before. Most importantly I have learned to not take my thyroid or any part of my body for granted.

I have worked with thousands of people over the years and my clients noticed specific changes in their lives and bodies when they began to bless and love their pain, each part of themselves

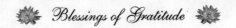

and their situation.   Many experienced a decrease in the pain levels and greater relaxation and peace of mind.

One of my clients, Mary, lost her job and was going through many changes.   Through the power of blessing her situation and being grateful for her life, she was able to release her fear and anxiety and become excited about all the new opportunities awaiting her.

One of the spiritual lessons I have learned and teach is that we are more than the obstacles in our life.

When we bless something it brings us into a state of love and gratitude which actually changes our frame of mind and perception from a negative state to a more positive one. It literally interrupts the way we see, feel and think about things and allows us to experience it differently.

If you are not comfortable with God as a reference point please substitute with Higher Power, Angels or any word or phrase that is appropriate and most comfortable for you.

Find out just how much your attitude and life can change by utilizing blessings and gratitude on a daily basis.   I hope it will help you get through rough times, as well as add great value and love to your life.

With love in my heart, make each blessing a ritual of gratitude for your mind, body, spirit and life.

Peace and blessings, Laurie

"Blessing imparts the quickening spiritual power that produces growth and increase.   To bless is to invoke good upon, to call forth the action of God."

– Charles Filmore

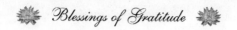
BLESSING OF GRATITUDE

I believe that gratitude is a very heart opening and life fulfilling spiritual practice.

No matter what is happening when you can stop and take a moment to think about all you are grateful for; you open yourself up to connect more deeply with your Divine Spirit and God.

This is a wonderful blessing to say whenever you want to tap into the feeling of gratitude.

I am truly grateful for all that I have in my life.

I give thanks for the people I love and for those who love me.

I bless my body and know I am the light and life of Spirit.

I bless and am grateful for happy times as well as difficult times.

I am open to see things that happen in my life as a blessing, even the so called bad things.   I am grateful for my work and for the people I work with.   I give thanks for all the spiritual guidance I receive.   Thank you God for all the blessings and love in my life.

BLESSINGS FOR EACH DAY, MORNING AND EVENING

How often do you start the day feeling tired or unmotivated?

When you start and end the day by blessing it you actually lift the vibration and set a more positive tone for that day and for your life. When you bless something it automatically brings you right into connection with your heart and spirit. Step out of the ordinary and start to create the life you were born to live. Spend each day being grateful for all you have and all the blessings in your life.

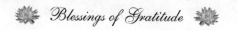

MORNING BLESSING

I am grateful for this day and for my life. I bless this day and know that it is a brand new beginning. Today is a day the Lord has made. I start this day knowing I am blessed and supported in all I do. I rejoice in the beauty that is all around me. I know this day is filled with laughter and joy. I open myself to receive and experience blessings and miracles showing up as a smile, kindness from a stranger, peace in my heart and abundance.

EVENING BLESSING

Thank you God, Divine Spirit for this day and this evening and another opportunity to love and to live life fully. I give thanks for all the people who have been a part of my day and I bless all the experiences I have had today. I know that my life is unfolding for my highest good. I am grateful for all that I have, all that I have learned today and for the clarity and direction in my life.

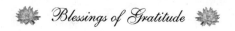

BLESSING YOURSELF

Are you used to blessing others when they sneeze?

How often do you actually take the time to bless yourself?

Do you spend time and energy judging, condemning and being angry with yourself; or feeling like you are not good enough?

You may choose to live your life feeling angry and fearful. Where does this get you?

It certainly does not get you anywhere if your intention is to live a positive, loving and healthy life. You can start to change this pattern and love yourself more by forgiving, blessing the positive and negative aspects and being grateful for whom you are on a daily basis. Blessing yourself will help you to bring greater good into your life by beginning to change your "self-talk" from negative to positive. Self forgiveness is an ingredient of self love.

I bless myself for just "being me." I am unique and there is no one else like me. I am made in the image and likeness of God. I forgive myself for anything I may have done in the past. I bless, accept and love my willingness to grow and be the best ME that I can be. I accept my positive and negative aspects now and am grateful for who I am and the difference that I make in the world.

Blessing God And The God Within You

So often we see ourselves differently than others see us. No matter what you may believe about yourself or got told by others, it is so important to remember that you are a spiritual being having a human experience. You are here in this lifetime to remember who you truly are and that you are made in the image and likeness of God. You are a loving presence and you do make a difference to those who you meet and know.

I bless and am so grateful for the divine spirit in my life
and the divine spirit that dwells within me. I know that
I am always surrounded, guided and loved no matter what
is happening. I know that I am never alone and I am the
expression of love and wholeness. I choose to always
remember the spiritual truth about myself and know that
all is good in my life, no matter what else is happening.

BLESSING THE CHILD WITHIN YOU

No matter how old you are, you have an inner child that lives within you. This inner child is that part of you that is innocent, playful, joyful, spontaneous, pure and loving. All your inner child wants is for you to love and accept him or her for who you are. If you have been too serious lately, spend time connecting and building a loving relationship with that child inside of you. You can do this by engaging in something you love doing or used to do when you were younger that you enjoyed. This can be playing a sport, building a sand castle or just doing something new and fun. Take the time to bless this wonderful part of you.

I bless, love and acknowledge my inner child knowing that he/she is such a special part of who I am. I am grateful for the joy, laughter, sweetness and innocence that my inner child brings to my life. I bless that child like part of me that knows how to have fun and enjoy the simple things in life.

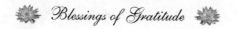

BLESSING EACH PART OF YOUR BODY

Did you know that your body is a sacred temple that houses your soul?

Do you ever feel angry or frustrated with your body because it is not doing what you want it to?

Did you know that you can store negative emotions in the cells of your body?

Take the time to bless and each part of your body and feel grateful for its amazing healing ability.   Whenever you acknowledge the good, beauty and intelligence of your body, you change the energy and allow it to transform, heal and flow.   Blessing each part of your body is also a way of loving and accepting yourself more deeply.   As you bless your body, send love and healing energy into each part.   Your body is calling out for you to love and nurture it.   This is a great opportunity to feel gratitude and build a deeper relationship with you in a more loving way from the inside out.

FACE, HEAD, HAIR, EYES, EARS AND NOSE

I bless and give thanks for all of my senses and my ability to hear, smell and see the beauty that is all around me. I thank God for all my senses.   I release and let go of any stress and tension that I am holding in my face, head, hair and scalp.   I bless my hair and am grateful for the beauty and softness of it.

MOUTH, TONGUE, TEETH, JAW AND THROAT

I bless my mouth, tongue, teeth, jaw and throat. I am grateful for the ability to speak, to smile, to laugh, to sing, to chew and swallow food and to express myself. It is easy to speak my truth and people want to hear what I have to say. I release and let go of any emotional stress, anger, frustration, fear and tension that I am holding in my mouth, jaw, teeth, tongue and throat. I joyfully express myself through my spoken word and through song.

ARMS, HANDS AND FINGERS

I bless my arms, hands and fingers for all they allow me to do. I am grateful for the ability to create with my hands and the gift of touch that my fingers provide. I thank God for the ability to reach out and touch someone's hand, cheek and to write and to be creative. I am grateful to be able to put my arms around someone I love and give them a hug.

LEGS, FEET AND TOES

I bless and I am so grateful for the ability to walk, move, dance and touch the earth. I am grateful to walk on a beach and feel the sand between my toes. I bless the miracle that my body is and all that I am able to do each and every day. I thank God for my strong legs and body. I am grateful for how my legs and feet allow me to move forward and take steps that bring me closer to God and to my purpose.

BACK, NECK AND SHOULDERS

I bless my back, neck and shoulders for allowing me flexibility and movement. I am grateful to God for every vertebra and to be able to stand, walk and sit. I am grateful for the support that my back, neck and shoulders provide for me. I bless each and every vertebra and every muscle along my spine. I joyfully release any burdens, fear, frustration, anger, stress or tension that I may be carrying in my back, neck and shoulders.

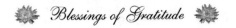

Torso – Chest, Diaphragm And Abdomen

I bless my chest, diaphragm and abdomen and am grateful for this part of my body. I release and let go of any tension and stress I may have in this area. I breathe deeply into my stomach and chest and feel more relaxed, balanced and at peace with every breath I take. I am grateful for the breath of life that feeds and nourishes every cell of my body.

Pelvis, Buttocks And Hips

I bless and thank my pelvis and hips for the ability to dance, move, sit and express my sensuality. I release and let go of any old shame, embarrassment, guilt and fear that I may be carrying in my pelvis and hips. I see the beauty and grace that my body is. I am grateful for this part of my body.

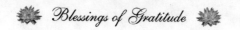

BLESSING EVERY ORGAN

Did you know that there is a direct connection between specific emotions and the organs?

We actually hold old emotional pain in the cells of our body. I have found in my work that people start to feel more balanced, healthier and calmer when they take the time to bless each organ. It is a way of creating a relationship from the inside out. Each organ has a physical function as well as an emotional, spiritual and mental connection.

This is a good opportunity to become more aware of your body and the emotions you may be unconsciously holding in your cells and giving yourself permission to release them.

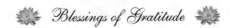
HEART

I bless and am grateful for the amazing job my heart does to pump the blood through my body. I thank God for the ability to feel, receive and express love, joy and compassion. I release and let go of any old feelings of hurt and forgive others and myself so that I may be more loving and joyful. I open my heart to express more of who I am and to experience a greater expansion and spiritual awakening.

LUNGS

I bless my lungs for the ability to breathe fully giving me the energy to do all that I do. I release and let go of any emotions such as sadness, loss and grief I may be carrying in my lungs that I have not yet expressed or acknowledged. I am grateful for the breath of God that breathes life into each and every cell every moment. I give thanks for the opportunity to continue to let go and trust myself more.

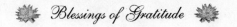

LIVER

I bless and am grateful for my liver and all it does to secrete bile, to digest fats, detoxify my body and keep me healthy. I feel more peace and balance inside. I let go of the past and release any feelings of anger and resentment toward myself or anyone else. I celebrate the passion and creativity within me.

GALL BLADDER

I bless my gall bladder and I am grateful for all that it does to store bile and aid in the digestion of fats. I release and let go of any frustration and irritability that I may be feeling and holding in my shoulders, back, head, jaw and body. I thank God for all that I have in my life and for the miracle and healing instrument that my body is.

KIDNEY

I bless and thank God for my kidneys. I give thanks for the incredible filtering system that they are. I am grateful for my vitality and aliveness. I release and let go of any fears that I may be holding in my body from the past that do not support my life and my well-being. I trust in my life, I trust in myself and am grateful for all that I have.

BLADDER

I bless and thank God for my bladder. I am grateful for the strength that it has to hold and release fluid. I release and let go of any emotional stress or negativity I may have stored in my bladder and in my body. I now allow my life to flow with ease and grace.

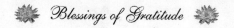

STOMACH

I bless and am grateful for the nourishment that my stomach provides by helping to digest my food easily and effortlessly. I release and let go of any nervousness, tension and stress I may have stored in my stomach. I thank God for my ability to experience emotional balance and love in my life.

SPLEEN

I bless my spleen and am grateful for all it does to keep my immune system strong and assist in blood and water balance. I release and let go of the need to worry about things I have no control over. It is easy for me to trust and feel good about my life and all that is unfolding.

PANCREAS

I bless and am grateful for my pancreas and the amazing job that it does to balance sugar and insulin, which is crucial for carbohydrate metabolism. I release and let go of anxiety and enjoy each and every moment. I thank God for the ability to experience the sweetness of life and live my life more fully. I deserve and am open to receive love and goodness in my life.

INTESTINES

I bless my intestines and I am so grateful and thankful for the amazing job that they do each and every day to digest and transport food and liquid as well as transmit and excrete waste products. I joyfully release and let go of any emotional stress, fear, tension or concern I may be storing in my intestines. I thank God for the ease, grace and flow of my digestive system, body and life. I am free to be me!

REPRODUCTIVE ORGANS

I bless my reproductive organs and thank God for the miracle and creation of life. I am grateful for the ability to feel and experience pleasure, passion and the joy of life itself.

GLANDS AND HORMONES

I bless all of my glands and hormones for keeping my body strong and healthy and my emotions in balance. I am grateful for the amazing job that my pituitary, thyroid, adrenal, thymus, prostate and pineal glands do for me each and every day. I release any stress that I may be carrying in these glands and I know that they are working beautifully in allowing me to do and be all that I can.

BLOOD AND LYMPHATIC SYSTEM

I bless and thank God for my blood and lymphatic system. I give thanks for my body being vital, energized and healthy, so that I can do and achieve all that I am here to do. I am grateful for good circulation all throughout my body.

BLESSING THE PARTS OF YOUR BODY
THAT ARE NO LONGER THERE

It is important to bless the parts of us that have been operated on, injured or surgically removed and are no longer there. By doing so it will help you to release and let go of any trauma, sadness, loss and emotional pain that is still in your body. It can help you to heal, accept yourself, feel whole again and live more fully in the present moment.

I bless and thank God for my life and for the parts of me that have been operated on, injured and are no longer there. I release any feelings of loss, guilt or sadness that I may have repressed. I embrace the whole of me and know that my body is miraculous and I am "perfect" just the way I am. I am grateful to be alive.

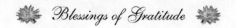

BLESSING THE PARTS OF YOUR BODY YOU DO NOT LIKE

So often we are not happy with our body and how we look. We think we will be happier and life will be better if we look different.

How do you feel about your body?

When we do not like parts of our body, we feel like there is something wrong and we actually cut off from loving ourselves and feeling whole. By blessing those parts you don't like, you are beginning the process of self love and acceptance. The changes to your self image can only come from changes made from the inside out. This is an important foundation for having healthy and loving relationships with yourself and others.

I bless my whole body and the parts I do not like knowing that they are all a part of me. I know that I am a unique emanation of God and therefore so is every part of my body. I am grateful for my body and now accept and love every part of me.

BLESSING EACH EMOTION

Our emotional side develops very early in our life.   For many of us we have felt very disconnected from our emotions as a way of protection or at times it can feel like they are out of control. It can even feel like you are carrying around heavy burdens when emotions have not been expressed.   Getting in touch with how you are feeling, acknowledging, blessing and releasing your emotions can really assist you in feeling lighter, more confident, balanced, peaceful and healthier.

I bless all of my emotions and know that they are there for a reason.   By recognizing and blessing my emotions it allows me to heal and release the past, be more open, and able to give and receive love.   I thank God and am grateful for the opportunity to bring more balance emotionally, physically, mentally and spiritually into my life and to stand in my own power.

BLESSING FOR WORRY

How often does your mind go into worrying about something or someone?

This can be an unconscious pattern that may cause quite a bit of struggle and negativity in your life. Worrying does not support your quality of life or support your happiness especially when you worry about something that is not in your control. Blessing what you are worrying about and being grateful for your life can help to change the way your mind processes the emotion of worry. It can help you to create more peace, health and harmony in your body, mind and soul by focusing on something more positive. Get in touch with what you are grateful for on a daily basis.

I bless my mind at all times and especially times of worry and doubt. I trust in God and know that all is in divine order in my life. I joyfully release all the worries over situations that I have no control and take right action with the situations that I can do something about. Each and every day I take control of my life and my thoughts. I feel empowered and am grateful for my life.

BLESSING FOR FEAR

Fear can feel so overwhelming, as though it is taking over our lives. We can feel like victims to our fear and our thoughts. I like to think of fear as "False Evidence Appearing Real." It is about experiencing thoughts that seem to be made up in your mind that were not real, even though they felt that way because of old belief patterns. Some fear is necessary, like the ones that keep us from walking alone on a dark street. We can often let fear stop us from really living, loving and enjoying life.

How does fear stop you in your life?

Start to bless your fear thoughts so that you can feel lighter and step back in control of creating a joyous and prosperous life. Spend time daily in gratitude for all the blessings in your life.

I bless all my fears and know that I always have power over my thoughts. I trust in God and am grateful for my life. I am grateful for the power of my intuition and trust in myself and I trust in what is right for me. I know that my intuition and inner knowing support my highest good. Every moment I choose to live more from the present and experience more wholeness, joy and love in my life.

BLESSING FOR FRUSTRATION

Do you ever feel tension in your shoulders, upper back, jaw and neck?

This can be signs of unexpressed frustration.

Ask yourself, "Is there anything I am feeling frustrated about?"

You may want to write it down. I have found that feeling frustrated keeps us stuck in the past and holds us back from feeling grateful and appreciating all the good things in our lives. As you release frustration you can begin to accept, love, enjoy and experience more in each moment. Blessing your frustration will help you to release those feelings and assist you to experience more energy and vitality physically, emotionally, mentally and spiritually.

I bless and release any frustration I may be feeling. I know I can choose to let the burden of it go and not hold it inside my body. I am grateful to God and know that my needs are met and all is flowing divinely in my life no matter what the outward appearance may be. I give myself permission to live in the now and to enjoy and accept each moment. As I let go of frustration I feel lighter and have more energy and vitality.

BLESSING FOR ANGER

It is important to express and acknowledge our feelings of anger.

Did you know that your anger can be expressed in a healthy way?

One of the ways to do this is by writing down and acknowledging your anger, disappointments and situations that did not work the way you wanted them to. When you give yourself permission to forgive, bless and accept your feelings of anger, you can begin to heal and release the past and move forward with ease, grace and passion. This is what living a life of gratitude, love and joy is all about.

I bless and am grateful for my anger as I know it is there to reveal more of what I need to heal and let go of within myself from the past. I release any anger that I may be feeling toward myself or anyone else. I embrace my feelings and bless the passion that lives within me. I am open to express my anger in a healthy and productive way for myself and all concerned. I feel spiritually held and supported and I am grateful for my life.

BLESSING FOR ANXIETY

Have you ever felt nervous and anxious?

Do you ever think about blessing your anxiety?

When you feel anxious it means you are living in the future or in the past and not in the present. You may feel disempowered by your anxiety, and just want it to go away. When you get anxious you may feel like a victim to that emotion and the effect it is having in your life. When you start to bless your feelings of anxiety and focus on being grateful for your life it can actually help you to feel more in control, trust yourself more, live fully in each moment and stand in your own power.

I bless my anxiety and am grateful for the opportunity to learn more about myself and to expand my confidence and intuition. I thank God for all the blessings in my life and know that I am perfect, whole and complete. I am grateful for the opportunity to release my fears, to stand in my power and be more present in my life in all that I do.

BLESSING FOR GRIEF

Experiencing grief and loss is a normal process of life. It can sometimes begin early in our childhood. For example; we can grieve if we did not get the love and acceptance we needed growing up. We not only grieve for the loss of a loved one, we grieve for our bodies ageing, for changes in our life including divorce, moving house, moving countries, relationships breaking up, getting ill, the loss of a job and so much more. Grief allows for a greater expansion of your heart. It opens your heart to feel more compassion and love for yourself and for others. It may not always feel good at times especially experiencing the variety of emotions that can come up such as anger, fear, numbness and sadness. Remember to love and take good care of yourself during the grieving process, and give yourself permission to acknowledge, express your feelings and ask for support.

I bless and am grateful for all the feelings I am experiencing as they are a reminder of my loving heart and how much I care. I know that as I express and release my feelings of grief over my losses, I open myself up to greater love and compassion for myself and for others. I let myself receive love and support from people that care about me. I am blessed and know that all is unfolding in divine order and I am spiritually held and loved.

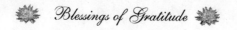

BLESSING FOR DEPRESSION

So many people experience feeling different degrees of depression. Feeling depressed can come from a chemical imbalance as well as from low self esteem, feelings of unworthiness, self hatred and feeling cut off spiritually.

What you need to remember is that whatever emotion you may be feeling is not who you are. Blessing your depression is like shining a light into a dark area. Where there is light there is more to see. It is important to forgive yourself for anything from the past that you may have done or felt bad about. Take the time to focus on gratitude for all you have and for the love and blessings in your life.

I bless my feelings of depression and know that I am more than these feelings. I am grateful for all that I have in my life and for all the people that love and care about me. I know I am never alone and I can ask and receive whatever help I need. I forgive myself and let go of any anger I may be feeling toward myself. I know that I am able to get through this time with ease and grace and all is unfolding for my highest good. I am willing to start accepting and loving myself more each day.
Thank you God for all the blessings in my life.

BLESSING FOR JOY

What are some of things that you like to do that bring you joy?

What stops you from feeling joyful?

When we judge ourselves or have low self esteem it can stop the flow of joy that we feel and want to express. Joy comes from our heart and divine spirit. It is a blessing to yourself and to others to express your joy and share it openly. Be like a little child and let your joy bubble up and shine through. You will find that as you do people will want to be with you and share in that energy.

Mother Teresa says: "God is joy. Joy is prayer. Joy is a sign of generosity. When you are full of joy, you move faster and want to go about doing well for everyone."

I bless my joy and know that it is an expression of my loving heart and when I am expressing my joy I am communing with the divine spirit. I am grateful to God for the feeling of joy and oneness flowing through my body and my life. I bless and forgive myself and I now choose to share my joy with everyone that I meet and know.

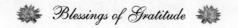

BLESSING FOR SHAME AND EMBARRASSMENT

Shame and embarrassment are two emotions that are seldom acknowledged. When we do not express these feelings and hold them inside of us, they can have a negative affect on our body-image, self-esteem, sexuality and relationships. I have found when these emotions are acknowledged and expressed people can sometimes experience a reduction in weight around the stomach, hip, thigh and buttocks areas.

I bless my feelings of shame and embarrassment and give myself permission to release them from my mind and body. I am grateful for who I am and know that I always do the best that I can. I bless my body and know it is sexy and beautiful just the way it is. I see myself the way God sees me. I feel good about myself and am grateful for my self confidence and self worth.

BLESSING FOR CONFUSION

How often do you think of blessing your confusion?

Confusion, although it may not feel so good at the time, is there for a reason. It is telling you to pay attention, to be still, trust yourself and know that something is changing within you. Take time when you are feeling confused to go within to ask what you need and listen for the answer. Confusion comes at times of change and transformation; it will lead to clarity and you will know exactly what to do next. If you want to feel better about yourself during this time; it may help to focus on what you are grateful for in your life.

I bless this time of confusion and know that it is there for a reason to reveal a new clarity and opportunity for me to grow. I know I have all I need to take the necessary steps to move forward. I trust in myself and in God and know that all is unfolding divinely, with ease, joy and grace. I am grateful for all the blessings in my life.

BLESSING YOUR RELATIONSHIPS

Each relationship we have teaches us so much about ourselves and is an opportunity for healing and spiritual growth. If your relationships do not seem to be easy and joyful you may be repeating old patterns. If this is the case, take time to look at your beliefs and see which ones are outdated and no longer supporting you. We can learn the most about life through our relationships with others whether they are intimate, professional or platonic.

I bless all my relationships and know that they are opportunities for me to learn more about myself, unconditional love and acceptance. I am so grateful for all the relationships in my life and I know that I deserve to be loved and cared for.

BLESSING YOUR IDEAL MATE

Do you ever wonder where your "perfect" partner is?

It can sometimes be a challenge to stay balanced and happy in ourselves when we are single and want to be in a relationship with our ideal mate. This is a good opportunity to release any fears from the past and to get clear on what your ideal partner would be like. The secret is to be all those things you want in a partner. Let us say that you want to meet someone who is loving, generous and healthy; then you need to be loving, generous and healthy. Be the person you want to attract into your life.

I am grateful for all that I have in my life. I know that I deserve a loving and intimate relationship. I am open and willing to be all that I am looking for in a partner. I release any fears and old beliefs about relationships and know that I am so worthy of love. Thank you God for bringing my ideal partner into my life for my highest good and the highest good of all concerned.

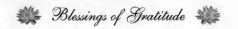

BLESSING YOUR INTIMATE RELATIONSHIP

Intimate relationships are such a sacred and blessed part of life. It can be easy sometimes to take our "significant other" for granted. Take the time to regularly bless your partner, your relationship and the intimacy that you share. This will support you to create more loving and positive energy with your partner, so that your relationship can continue to grow and expand on all levels. Take the time to bless your lovemaking. This helps to make it a more sacred, loving and spiritual experience.

I bless my relationship and am grateful for the intimacy that my beloved and I share together. I bless our lovemaking and know we are constantly lifted to higher levels of love and connection. I thank God for the blessing that is my relationship. I am grateful for all the love that is in my life.

BLESSING YOUR EX-PARTNERS

Whether or not you have ended your relationships in a positive way, it is good to keep your heart open and to start a new relationship from that loving place. One of the ways to do this is by blessing and forgiving your ex-partners. When you bless your ex-partners you let go of the negative emotions and hurt from the past and allow for more love, grace and joy to flow into your heart and life. Blessing your past relationships allows you to be more of who you are today in your current relationships.

I bless and forgive my past partners. I am grateful for all of my experiences and relationships as I have grown and learned so much more about myself and about love. I know that each and every relationship teaches me more about myself. I joyfully release past partners, make peace with the past and live more fully each day.

BLESSING THE UNCERTAINTY AROUND YOUR RELATIONSHIPS AND YOUR LIFE

How do you respond in times of uncertainty?

For a lot of people uncertainty can bring up feelings of fear and doubt. It can be easy to avoid making decisions during these times because it feels uncomfortable. This is a good time to meditate and quiet your mind as much as possible so that you can listen to your inner guidance and trust in your heart what is right for you. When you bless the uncertainty it may help you to respond and take action from a place of balance than acting out of fear.

I bless this time of uncertainty around my relationship and life knowing that it is bringing about positive change and growth. I accept where I am and know that all is coming into a clear perspective. I bless and know that all is good and is unfolding in divine order. I thank God for this opportunity to be still, to trust more and to listen to the divine spirit within me.

BLESSING FOR SEPARATION

When we separate from our partner, family and children it can be a most painful time of change for all concerned. Separation can also be a blessing as it is an opportunity to love and trust yourself on a deeper level. It can be a very powerful time of personal and spiritual growth and insights. Yes, many fears may come up for you and it is important to have faith and believe that all is unfolding for your highest good and the highest good of all your loved ones.

I bless this time and know that it is all unfolding in divine order for the highest good of all concerned. I release my fear, doubt and uncertainty and put my trust and faith in myself and in God. I bless each and every member of my family and know we have all the support we need. I am grateful for all the love and support I have in my life. I am grateful for me!

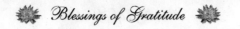

BLESSING FOR DIVORCE

Divorce can be a very scary and difficult time. On another level it is an opportunity for change, letting go of the old and stepping forth into a new adventure. Blessing this time allows you to release negative feelings and emotions such as anger, fear, doubt and uncertainty and to enter into a deeper spiritual time of trust, self acceptance and faith. It is a time to reach out and ask for support and to allow people to be there for you. Take the time on a daily basis to focus on all that you are grateful for.

I bless this time of change and the new journey that I am embarking on. I ask for this period of change to be filled with ease, grace, support and love for myself and all concerned. I thank God for this opportunity to grow and become more of who I am. I know that all is working for my good and all is unfolding in my life in divine order and joy. I am grateful and trust in the knowing that all my needs are met and that I am deeply loved.

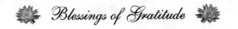

BLESSING YOUR FAMILY AND LOVED ONES

It can be easy sometimes to take our family and loved ones for granted. We may think they will always be around and when we get angry we can sometimes take it out on those closest to us. Be grateful for the time you share with family and cherish each moment. Even in conflict, family and loved ones can be our greatest teachers. Let the people you love know how you feel about them while they are still alive even if you have differences with them.

I am so grateful for and bless each member of my family and all my loved ones and wish the very best for them always. I feel so blessed for all the love that is in my life. I thank God for the wonderful people who love me and who I love.

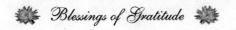

BLESSING YOUR PARENTS

Whatever your relationship may be with your parents or the people who raised you; whether they are alive or have died, it is never too late to forgive and create more love and peace with them inside of your heart.

The relationship we have with our parents has a direct effect unconsciously on each and every relationship we have, especially the intimate ones.

Have you ever felt like your partner reminded you of one of your parents?

If there are areas of conflict or separation with your parents it can show up in your relationships and give you an opportunity for healing to occur. Blessing your parents helps to expand your heart, live fully in the present and create more love in your life.

I bless and thank God for my parents and all they have given to me and taught me in my life. I am grateful for all that I have learned and for my mother and father being my greatest teachers even in hard times. I bless my life and I know it is my responsibility to create more love, success and joy in my life.

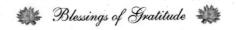

BLESSING SINGLE PARENTS

It is not always an easy road being a single parent and being able to stay balanced in doing so. Remember that you cannot do it all. It is important to ask for whatever help and support you may need. Make it a priority to take good care of your self, so that you do not get exhausted and burned out.

I honor and pay deep respect to all parents and especially single parents who are doing the best they can to raise and love their children. If you are a single parent or parent say this blessing to yourself personally using "I." It can help to give you more inner strength and peace during challenging times.

I bless myself for being the best role model I can be and for doing my best to raise healthy and loving children no matter what is happening. I bless and thank God for single parents and parents, who have the greatest job of all; being great role models and raising healthy, happy, confident and loving children. I am grateful for my life.

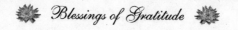

BLESSING YOUR EXTENDED FAMILY

This blessing has special significance and meaning for me personally. I now have the first hand experience of being part of an extended family. There are a wide range of emotions, feelings, adjustments and compromises involved in the dynamics of an extended family. It takes unconditional love, clear communication, a lot of patience and daily blessings to help create a supportive home environment for everyone involved. Having an attitude of gratitude can certainly help to see things in a more positive way.

I bless and thank God for each member of my extended family. I am grateful for all that I am learning about myself and my ability to communicate clearly. I call forth and know that I receive all the spiritual support and guidance I need to be more loving and compassionate on a daily basis. I am grateful for this new family in my life.

BLESSING YOUR CHILDREN

We can learn so much from children about Spirit, God, how to live in the moment, express feelings, play and be honest. All you have to do is watch a child play and you see all the wonder in their eyes when they look at or hold an ant or flower. They are pure, innocent and just want to love and be loved. If you do not have your own children, you can say this blessing for all children.

I bless and acknowledge my children for who they are and the love and joy they bring to my life. They are truly a blessing from God and I am grateful for everything that they teach me each and every day. I bless them with good health, joy, love and happiness.

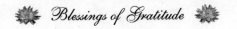

BLESSING YOUR SIBLINGS

How is your relationship with your siblings?
Is there anything you need to forgive them for?

Just as your parents are teachers in your life, so are your brothers and sisters. What happens in your immediate family plays a vital part in your other relationships in life. In what ways can you make your relationships with your siblings even better?

Life is so very precious. Take the time to be grateful and let your siblings know how much they mean to you and how much they are appreciated.

I bless my siblings and know that whether we get along
or not we are great mirrors and teachers for one another.
I forgive them and myself for any negative feelings I may
be carrying from the past. I am grateful for all the times
they have been there for me when I needed them.
I thank God for my family and continue to love, support
and open my heart to them and to others.

BLESSING YOUR FRIENDS

Friendship is such an important part of one's life. Think about the friends that you feel close to and love. Take the time on a regular basis to bless, acknowledge and appreciate them for who they are. Let go of any judgment that may get in the way of your friendships. Let your friends know that they make a difference in your life.

I bless and thank God for the friends in my life. I am grateful for all the unconditional love and support I have and how special my friendships are to me. I am grateful for my wonderful friends for who they are and for all they have brought to my life.

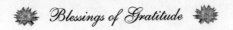

BLESSING YOUR FRIENDS WHO ARE
NO LONGER IN YOUR LIFE

We are blessed with people coming into our lives even if it is for a very short time. We all have something valuable to learn and share with each other. Recognize and be grateful for the spiritual gifts you have received from friends who have been in your life.

I thank God and bless all the wonderful friends that have been in my life. I know that each and every person has added a special dimension of love and caring that has made me who I am today and made my life more meaningful. I am grateful for the difference that I made in their life as well.

BLESSING PEOPLE THAT YOU ARE IN CONFLICT WITH

Do you ever find yourself in conflict with someone and have trouble letting the negative feelings go?

The truth is that if you are holding on to anger, resentment or negativity, the only person that it affects is YOU. It does not affect the other person. It is hard to be present and move forward without struggle when you are carrying emotional burdens from the past.

By changing the way you look at a situation, being grateful for and blessing the conflict can help you to release the negative feelings and feel more peaceful inside.

I bless and forgive the person/situation that I have been feeling conflicted about. I choose now to release and let go of any negative thoughts and energy that I may have been holding onto. I am grateful for each moment I can release negative thoughts and feelings. By letting go I know that I am making my life better. I feel grateful for this experience and all that I have learned from it and the changes that I have made within myself. I know that I am a better person for coming back to a place of peace and love inside of me. Thank you God for all the opportunities I am given to grow and learn more about love and acceptance.

BLESSING FOR SOMEONE WHO IS DYING

The process of dying is a holy and sacred one. It is the releasing of the physical body as we know it, as well as a new adventure and journey for our soul. It is an opportunity to let people you love know your feelings and to say whatever you need to say for completion. It is important to release any fears you might be feeling or holding inside for yourself or your loved one. It is a time of getting in touch with those loved ones that have died and feeling the love and support from the spiritual realm. If this is for someone you love, put their name in the blessing.

I bless this sacred process of transition that I am going through or someone I love is going through. I know that I am and they are held in the loving arms of God at all times. I release and let go of any fear I may be feeling. I embrace this journey that I am on and know that I have made a difference to all the people I have loved and touched. I am grateful to know that my/their spirit lives on in the hearts and memories of all those I or my loved one leaves behind and my love stays with them until we meet again.

BLESSING YOUR LOVED ONES WHO HAVE DIED

There are a variety of emotions we can experience with the death of a loved one. Take the time to acknowledge what you are feeling and get the support you need. Whatever you may be feeling, it is important to remember that life is eternal and the spirit and memory of your loved ones lives on forever in your heart. You can honor their life by remembering the love you shared together and how they touched your life and the difference you made in their life.

I bless all those that have gone before me and know they are free. I know their love and spirit are always with me, in my heart. I thank God for the love and grace with which they surround me. I rejoice in the beautiful memories that we shared and am grateful for the time that we had together.

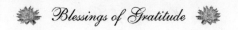

Blessings For Miscarriage,
Stillbirth And The Loss Of A Child

This kind of loss is so important to acknowledge and express even if it happened years ago.   There may be a deep place of emptiness inside that does not seem to go away.   One of the ways to express and heal the loss of a child is by blessing the child, yourself and the experience.   It is important to get whatever emotional support you may need to help you through this loss and to know that you are not alone.

I bless the loss of my child and know that his/her spirit is with God and is with me in my heart.   I am grateful for the blessings that my child has brought to my life and all we have shared.   I forgive, release and let go of any guilt, grief and sadness that may be in my body.   I give thanks for the beautiful spirit of my child and know I am surrounded with divine grace and love.

BLESSING YOUR ANCESTORS

You may not be aware of or know how much of a blessing and influence your ancestors have in your life spiritually.

The core essence of who you are today has a lot to do with your past experiences and with your ancestors. It can be easy to go through life feeling alone and needing some direction. We can call forth the energy, love and wisdom of our ancestors to support, guide and direct us anytime we are in need. You can do this through your dreams, in meditation and through this blessing.

I bless my ancestors, those who have come before me. I am grateful for the knowledge and wisdom they impart to me on so many levels unconsciously and consciously. I thank God for who I am and all the ways my ancestors have blessed my life. I know I am never alone. I am open and available to receive the love, support and wisdom they have to share with me.

BLESSING HUMANKIND AND PEOPLE YOU DO NOT KNOW

Have you ever met a stranger and felt like you had known them for a long time?

We often hear how small the world really is when our paths cross with others we may know or are meeting again.

As human beings we can experience judgment or prejudice against someone who is different from us out of protection and fear. We are all connected in one way or another and are all God's children no matter our culture, religion, color, where we live or if we happen to be different in some way.

I bless all people regardless of race, color and religion. I release and let go of my fears and judgments toward others. I choose to be kind and tolerant and to see the best in people. I am willing to recognize that each and every person is a child of God as I am.

BLESSING FOR ANIMALS

Animals can be great teachers, guides and divine channels of love. We can learn so much about unconditional love from our animals. Animals tend to have a keen awareness and understanding of healing and energy. They know instinctively what we are feeling and when we need closeness and tender loving care. They also know when we are afraid. They can teach us a lot about how to play and be in the moment, just as children do.

I bless all the animals large and small, wild and tame. I give thanks for those animals that fly, those that swim in the sea and those that live on the ground. I am grateful for the divine beauty and grace that is the animal kingdom. Knowing that they are part of the oneness of creation, I thank God for all animals.

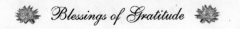

BLESSING YOUR CAT

Cats are wonderful, alive, joyful, loving and playful animals. They have so much to teach us about how to play and to do the things we enjoy. They absolutely ask for what they need and are open to receiving what they need. They are an example of unconditional love and are great sources of comic relief.

I bless my cat/cats and am grateful for all the gifts, playfulness and joy they bring into my life. I am grateful for them being my "angels in fur coats" and great companions. I thank God for the cats in my life and for beautiful animals that cats are.

BLESSING YOUR DOG

Dogs have been known as our best friends. They are affectionate, loyal, loving and always there when we need them. They intuitively know when we are not feeling well and when we need some extra loving care. Dogs are always there to greet you when you come home and are so happy to see you. They are great teachers of unconditional love, healing and joy.

I give great thanks and bless my dog/dogs for all the love, joy and companionship they bring into my life each and every day. I thank God for the love of my dog/dogs and I feel so blessed and grateful to have them in my life.

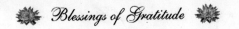

BLESSING YOUR ANIMALS WHO HAVE DIED

Animals are such a special and important part of our life. For so many people their pets become like children to them. When our beloved pet dies, it is important to let ourselves grieve the loss and to say goodbye. Take the time to bless and thank your divine animal for all the love they have brought into your life. Give yourself the permission to grieve and get whatever support you feel is important for you to get through this time of loss.

I bless and thank God for my beloved friend and companion. I am grateful that this beautiful pet came into my life and shared so much love with me. I know his/her spirit will always be with me.

BLESSING YOUR MIND AND THOUGHTS

Did you know that what you think creates who you are and has a direct effect on what you experience?

Your mind can work for you or against you.   Creating heaven on earth has a lot to do with your beliefs, attitudes and thought patterns.   Your life can transform when you choose the thoughts that best support you and all concerned.   As stated in the Bible, *"Be ye transformed by the renewing of your mind."*

When you bless something and feel grateful for it; you begin to alter your thought patterns and this enables you to choose thoughts that are more positive and supportive.

I thank God and bless all my thoughts. I consciously choose thoughts that are positive, loving, supportive and enhance my life. I know that I am in charge of my thoughts, attitudes and perceptions. I am grateful for the ability that my mind has to think, remember, imagine, comprehend, create and learn new things. I choose to be the master of my mind and to see things that happen as a blessing.

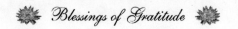

BLESSING AND FORGIVING YOUR PAST

Do you ever spend time thinking about and reacting to things that happened in the past?
Do you carry regrets from the past with you?

When you do this you are literally bringing the past into your present reality. This can keep you from completely enjoying your life now!

Bless and forgive situations from your past so that you can experience more joy in your life now. This sometimes can feel very hard and requires a lot of practice and awareness. Be patient and keep on loving yourself through this. You cannot change what happened in the past, however you can begin to see it differently in your mind and be grateful for all that it has taught you and who you are today. This can help you to live more fully in each moment.

I bless my past for all that I have learned and experienced about myself and my life. I am grateful for the journey I have been on and know that it has brought me to where I am today. Thank you, God for giving me patience, self-love and understanding. I am grateful for all the blessings in my life and all the people who have helped me along the way. I am willing to forgive and release past painful situations and I embrace each present moment with love, joy and an open heart.

BLESSING TIMES OF CHANGE

Change is a natural part of life and when we fight against it, like fighting against a current, all we get is tired and worn out. Blessing the changes happening in your life allows you to move through them with more grace, joy and ease no matter what they are. Times of change can give you a chance to expand yourself spiritually and experience new things by stepping out of what feels comfortable. The blessings that come from times of change can be many including, expanding your perception of yourself, allowing you to trust more and opening up to experience new opportunities.

I bless and am grateful for all the changes in my life, knowing they are opportunities for me to trust, grow and become a better person. I call forth ease and grace in times of change and know that I always have all the support I need. I welcome in the new and know that all is taking place for my highest good and the highest good of all concerned. I know I am never alone, I am always supported and am grateful to God for all of my blessings.

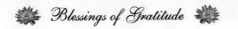

BLESSING FOR PUBERTY

This is a time of great change physically, emotionally, mentally and spiritually. It may be a vulnerable and scary time because your body and voice are changing and the sensations and emotions are so new. It is a time of exploration of one's own body and a time of journeying from childhood to adolescence. It can feel like a confusing time when support, patience, understanding and love are required.

I bless this time of change, growth and exploration. I am grateful for this journey from childhood to adulthood. I know that I can have all the love, guidance, understanding and support that I need and am open to receive it. I thank God for this time of growth, establishing self confidence and becoming my own person.

BLESSING FOR MENSTRUATION

This is a very profound and sacred time for young girls marking the passage from childhood to womanhood. Creating a positive and loving experience for your daughter is very important. This can be a challenging and scary time because of the emotional and physical changes that can occur. Ask her what you can do for her and what she needs to make it a special, supportive and memorable experience. For women, take this time to bless and honor your own menses and body each month as it is a very spiritual and sacred time.

I bless this time of menstruation and rite of passage for girls experiencing their first menses. I bless and am grateful for my body and the emotional and physical changes that are taking place. I bless each and every month of menstruation and know that all is flowing in my life with perfect rhythm, ease and grace.

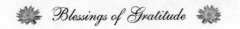
BLESSING DURING PREGNANCY

During pregnancy you may experience a variety of body changes and different emotions. It is a wonderful opportunity to connect on a deeper loving level spiritually with your unborn child and letting him/her know how loved they are. Take the time to release and let go of any fears you may have around being a parent and childbirth. It is a time to celebrate life and the amazing ability your body has to create and carry another living being inside of you.

I bless and thank God for all the amazing changes my body is making to support and give life to my child. I bless and thank my hormones for all that they do to keep me and my baby balanced and healthy. I am grateful for the miracle of love and life that is happening each and every day inside of me. I bless this beautiful child of God and know that all is well.

BLESSING FOR ADOPTION

Adopting a child is a very joyous and exciting time for a couple and family. It can sometimes be a stressful process. It is also a celebratory time that marks a new passage and a new beginning of love and life for the parents, child and family. Bless all of the people involved with this adoption and all the feelings and experiences that may arise in this time.

I bless and thank God for this beautiful child, his/her birth parents and our new family. I bless the agency, birth parents and everyone involved with this adoption. I know that this process is unfolding with ease, joy, love and grace. The highest good is taking place for all of us right here and right now. I bless our beautiful child/children and the loving family that we have.

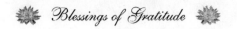

BLESSING FOR MENOPAUSE

What is important to you at this stage of your life?
What new things would you like to pursue?

Menopause is a powerful time of releasing the past, letting go of monthly menstruations and saying goodbye to a part of one's life. It is a time of physical and emotional change when women can feel quite vulnerable and sensitive. It can be a time when you feel emotionally like you are on a roller coaster. Be gentle and loving with yourself and ask for what you need.

It is important to remember that from a spiritual point of view you are stepping into a new stage of becoming a "wise" woman and elder. It is a great opportunity to get to know your body and self on a whole new level. Take the time to be grateful for all you have in your life. Bless yourself and your body during this time of change.

I bless this time of menopause and all the changes that are happening inside and out. I thank God for this new stage of freedom in my life. I bless all the emotions that I am experiencing. I am so grateful for all the wisdom and knowledge that I have acquired throughout my life. I am grateful and feel blessed for this opportunity to come back into balance and step into a greater awareness of my love, light and beauty as a woman.

BLESSING NURSES, HEALERS, THERAPISTS AND CAREGIVERS

The role of the caregiver is quite a large one. It takes someone who is extremely compassionate and dedicated to helping others to do this kind of work.

We are all caregivers in one way or another whether it is with raising children, working in the health profession, loving and caring for our family, our animals and caring for the environment. Take the time to care for yourself and keep your energy and body balanced so that you can avoid burnout and continue to enjoy your work. Remember to get the love and nurturing that you need.

I bless and thank God for all the nurses, healers, therapists and caregivers that help others in a loving and supportive way. I am grateful for all they do to make this world a better place. I bless my open and loving heart for all that I do to care for others. I choose to take great care of myself each and every day as well as being there for others.

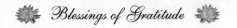

BLESSING FOR ILLNESS

What if your illness was actually a blessing in disguise?

I believe that our illnesses and our pain are here for a specific reason and purpose. We can begin to discover the blessing during this time as we step out of our fear and begin to experience the positive changes and opportunities that can come from an illness or ill health. These changes may include slowing down, recognizing our inner strength, learning how to receive love and accepting ourselves more than ever before.

Notice what happens for you when you focus on gratitude and start blessing your illness and seeing it as a blessing. Take this time to love yourself more, reach out and get the love, help and support from others that you require.

I bless my illness knowing that it is in my life for a higher purpose. I am grateful for all that I am learning and the opportunity to love and accept myself more. I bless my illness and love each part of my body. I give thanks to God for all the help, love and support that I have and for my spiritual journey. I am grateful to know that I am not alone and am spiritually guided, loved and supported through this and every experience.

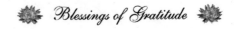

BLESSING FOR PAIN

Did you know that your body has a message for you and pain is a way to get your attention?

Your pain may need you to know something and is a signal that your body is out of balance. I believe that pain is a messenger. The more that you resist your pain, the more it will persist. Blessing your pain is an important step in allowing your body to shift, change and become more balanced. Take the time to stop, breathe deeply and tune into what your body is telling you and then you may discover what it needs.

I bless my pain and understand it is here for a specific reason and has an important message for me. I am open and willing to hear the messages that my body has for me and to take better care of myself. I am grateful to God for the opportunity that my pain gives me to know, listen and love myself more.

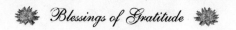

BLESSING YOUR MEDICINE

Blessing your medication before you take it you can help lift the vibrational frequency to help your body digest and absorb it in the best way possible for healing to occur.   Since everything is energy, you can create a more positive environment for your mind and body by blessing your medications every time you take them. This also includes vitamins and minerals.

I bless my medications and know that I am lifting it to a higher frequency to assist my body in its healing process. I am grateful for the way the medications I am taking support my body on a cellular level to relieve pain, come back into balance and stay healthy.

BLESSING DIFFICULT TIMES

Have you ever experienced something good and unexpected coming out of a so-called "bad" situation?

It may sound strange to think of blessing difficult times because it can be easy to get caught up in the negativity of the situation. When you begin to bless this experience and yourself, you are more open to respond and react in a way that is positive and allows new opportunities to occur. Take this time to be grateful for your inner strength, courage and all you are learning.

I bless all that is happening in my life and know there is a reason and a higher purpose for it all. I release and let go of any feelings of fear, struggle and negativity I may be experiencing. I am grateful for the spiritual and personal growth taking place in my life here and now. I choose to see, act and respond to this time in a way that is most supportive to me and my loved ones. I am open and willing to see the blessing in this situation. I give thanks for my life.

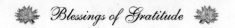

BLESSING YOUR SURGERY AND OTHER TREATMENTS

There may be a lot of fear, stress and anxiety associated with surgery and medical treatments. You may feel out of control especially if some of your questions and concerns have not been addressed or if you had negative experiences in the past.

One of my clients had a lot of fear associated with her past surgeries and spending time in the hospital. I was with her the morning of surgery and together we blessed her upcoming surgery and saw it going smoothly and that her body healed and recovered so quickly. She came out of the recovery room in such good shape that she was able to go home within a couple of hours after surgery. When she got home her family marveled at how good she looked and how good she felt. Blessing your surgery and treatments can help you to release your fears and anxiety, experience it from a positive point of view, feel more at peace and assist your body in its recovery process.

I bless the surgeon and doctor's hands, all the nurses and staff working with me. I am grateful to know that God is always with me, surrounding, uplifting, loving and healing. My life is truly in "good" hands. I know that my body has an incredible intelligence and knows how to heal. I am relaxed and feel a deep peace inside of me. All is unfolding with ease and grace. I am healthy and renewed.

73

BLESSING FOR CHEMOTHERAPY, RADIATION AND OTHER TESTS

It is normal to get worried and frightened when taking tests or having treatments, especially ones that may lead to an uncertain outcome.   This has a lot to do with feelings of vulnerability, fear and helplessness.

Do you ever notice your mind being focused on the worst possible scenario?

This can create a stressful environment in your body and blessing your body and specific test you are having can help you to focus on the positive.   Blessing whatever test or treatment you are taking can help you to release fear and stay more relaxed and peaceful. It is also helpful for your peace of mind to find out whatever information you need to know.   Remember to keep focusing on all you are grateful for in your life and the blessing that can come from every situation.

BLESSING FOR CHEMOTHERAPY, RADIATION AND OTHER TESTS

I bless the chemotherapy, any other treatment and all those involved in this process. I let go of any fear or stress that I may be feeling. I bring myself back to the present moment and I know that God is present and divine healing is taking place in every cell of my body. I know that as the drug goes into my body it turns into light and supports the healing process. I am grateful that my body temple is getting stronger and all is in divine order. I bless and thank God for the tests that I need to take knowing that all is unfolding for my highest good, whatever that might be. I am grateful for my life.

BLESSING FOR DISEASE

What support do you need right now?

There are a wide range of diseases that people have to live with on a daily basis. This blessing encompasses all diseases and disorders including: heart disease, AIDS, digestive disorders, diabetes, lupus, emphysema and whatever else you may be experiencing.

As with any illness it can be a time of experiencing a variety of emotions such as despair, frustration, anger, impatience and fear especially when it is chronic and there does not seem to be a "cure" for what is ailing us. Sometimes people can feel disconnected spiritually and want to withdraw. It is important to take time on a daily basis to pray, meditate, bless and send love and healing energy to your body, yourself and to whatever you may be experiencing.

Give yourself permission to receive the support you need for your mind, body and spirit during this time to help you feel more peaceful and relaxed.

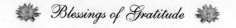

BLESSING FOR DISEASE

I bless and send loving energy to my body and present situation. I give thanks for all the love and support I have around me. I am grateful for my faith, inner strength and courage. I give myself permission to express what I am feeling, to forgive and to let any negative thoughts and burdens to be lifted from me now. I thank God for all of my blessings and for all I am learning about myself and my body. I am willing to receive more love and healing energy than I have ever experienced before. I trust that all is unfolding for my highest good and that I have all the patience and inner peace that I require.

BLESSING FOR CANCER

How would your life be different if you could bless your cancer and be willing to see it as a blessing, whether you are healed or not?

This can be quite challenging, especially when we are first diagnosed. So many people are experiencing a lot of pain and fear associated with having cancer. I know that I did.

What if you could see this as an opportunity to embrace your fears, ask for support, and get more in touch with your faith and inner strength?

It was quite a shock to me when I was told I had cancer and I had a hard time at first recognizing all the ways it was a blessing in my life. The blessings I experienced included an opportunity to slow down, let people be there for me and receive more love.

For many it can be a time of receiving love and nurturing from others. If you are someone who has always been the caregiver and have had a hard time asking for help and letting yourself receive, now is your chance. People who care about you do want to be there to unconditionally love and support you.

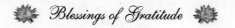

BLESSING FOR CANCER

I bless my cancer and send loving thoughts and energy into every cell of my body. I release and let go of my emotional burdens, fear, guilt, resentment and negativity that I may have repressed. I am grateful for this opportunity to surrender to Divine Spirit for love, healing, receiving from others and letting go of my need to control. I deserve to be loved and to get the help I need. I am open and grateful for it all now. I allow my mind and body to be healed and I thank God for all the grace and love that surrounds me.

BLESSING FOR EATING DISORDERS

Do you ever feel like you are not quite right the way you are? What do you need to forgive yourself for?

For those people struggling with any kind of eating disorder, it is so important to get loving help and support for your body, mind, emotions and spirit. It can be difficult sometimes to admit that we have an eating disorder and need help. Take the time to be gentle and loving with yourself. One of the ways to do this is by blessing your body and every aspect of yourself every day, even the parts you do not like. It is good to have some kind of daily spiritual practice that nurtures your body, mind and spirit. This can be listening to beautiful music, meditating, praying, spending time in nature, being creative or whatever you enjoy that feeds your soul.

I bless myself, my body and I accept more balance, vitality, love and peace inside of me now.

I forgive myself for anything that may have hurt me or hurt others from the past. I embrace life and thank God for all the love and support I have. I am ready to love myself more and put myself as a priority. I am grateful for my body and for who I am. I choose now to see myself in a whole new way. I choose to see myself as God sees me.

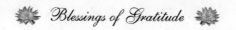

BLESSING YOUR DOCTORS

Is there anything you need your doctor to know about you to help you the most?

It is your body and is important for you to begin to trust in your intuition or as I call it "your inner knower" on what is best for you. Take the time to ask questions until you get the answers you require. Find the right doctor that will listen to you and work along with you.

Your doctors are here for a reason and even though you may not always agree with them, it is important to work together in a harmonious partnership. Blessing your doctors can create a healthier, more open relationship with them. You are a team and therefore need to work together in a way that supports the whole of you (which includes your body, mind, emotions and spirit).

I am grateful for my doctors and bless them for all the knowledge they have and for the willingness to listen to me, work with me and provide the needed resources for my healing. I trust myself and my intuition. I know that the doctor I choose to work with is easy to communicate with and respects where I am coming from. I am grateful for the divine healer inside of me and the intelligence of my body. I bless all the medical staff and know they are all part of God's team and are working together for my highest good.

BLESSING YOUR FOOD

When you bless your food, whether it is food that you eat at a restaurant or food you prepare yourself, it helps to lift the frequency and vibration of it. Lifting the vibration of the food we eat through our conscious awareness, thoughts and blessings enables our body and digestive system to become more vital, energized and vibrant by putting loving and healing energy into it. Take the time to bless and be grateful for your food as you prepare it and as you eat it.

I bless and am grateful for this food that I am cooking and about to eat. I know that this food nurtures and energizes every cell of my body. I appreciate all that it took to get this food to me. I bless the restaurant and all the people who had something to do with creating this meal. I know that my food is filled with divine love, energy and light. I thank God for all I have.

BLESSING NATURE'S BEAUTY – BLESSINGS FOR THE EARTH

We are surrounded by the richness of the earth and the exquisite home it provides for each of us. I am always in awe of how sacred and beautiful nature is and the magnificence of sunrises, sunsets, trees, and majestic mountains as well as the awesome power of the ocean, rivers and waterfalls. Nature and all it has to offer truly is a holy place and one that needs to be cherished and taken care of. We are the caretakers of the earth and it is up to each of us to care for the earth, our home and sanctuary.

I bless and thank you "Mother Earth" for the beauty that is all around me in the ocean, rivers, lakes, mountains, rocks trees, gardens, sunsets and sunrises. I am grateful for the beautiful home that is provided for me and for all of us. I am grateful! for the air that I breathe, the water I drink, the sky, moon, sun and stars. Each and every day I rejoice in the grace of God's creation.

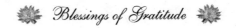

BLESSING YOUR CAR AND TRANSPORTATION

Whether you have your own car or take public transportation, it can be easy to take them for granted.

How often do you think about blessing your car or mode of transportation?

Do you feel grateful for your car before you start driving it, and grateful when it gets you to where you are going?

When we feel grateful for what we have it opens us up energetically to receive more in our lives.

Take the time to bless the mode of transportation that you do take each day.

I thank you God for my vehicle of transportation. I bless it and feel grateful for the way it gets me to where I need to be with comfort and safety. I am so grateful for my car and how it supports my life and the life of my loved ones.

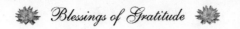

BLESSING YOUR HOME

Sometimes the environment we live in may not be as healthy as it could be. How much clutter do you have around your home? Keeping the energy clear in your home will help to improve your health and well-being. One way of doing this is by cleaning out the old and giving away what you no longer need. One of my clients had trouble sleeping at night and always woke up feeling tired. I suggested she try blessing each room and getting rid of things she no longer needed. She was able to sleep more soundly and felt rested and relaxed when she woke up.

To set the intention and create a sacred environment, you can light candles, burn incense, play music or whatever works for you while you are blessing every room. As you bless each room, think about the qualities you want to have there; like peace, love, creativity and harmony and put those into the blessing. Notice if your home feels any different and make this a regular ritual.

I thank you God and am grateful for my wonderful home and all that I have. I bless the roof over my head and each room of my home, the back and front yard. I know that my home gives me and my family all that I/we need to live, feel relaxed, renewed, creative, loved and supported. I know that the space I live in is sacred and blessed.

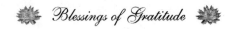

BLESSING YOUR OFFICE

When you think about your office or workplace, what does it represent to you?
What is the kind of environment you want to work in?

If there is any clutter in your office (like papers stacked up high and old files you no longer need), it may be blocking your creativity and finances from flowing freely.   Take the time to regularly de-clutter your workplace and create a healthy environment.   Blessing and being grateful for your office is a good way to create a more productive environment for you to work in.

I bless and am grateful for my creative abilities and financial abundance in my life.   It is easy for me to clear the clutter and allow my creative energy to flow freely in my life. I am grateful for all that I have and all that I do.   I know that my office and work environment supports me on all levels to do the best job that I can.

BLESSING THE WORK THAT YOU DO

How often do you take the time to be grateful for the work you do?

No matter what your work is, you are there for a reason.

Ask yourself, what can I do today to make the work that I do more meaningful?

What difference do I make to others?

If you are unhappy with the work you are doing and unclear about what you want to be doing, blessing your work may give you more motivation, clarity and direction.   Remember that your attitude can make all the difference.   Gratitude can really help us to see things in a more positive way and feel more motivated and productive.

I give thanks, appreciate and feel very blessed for the work that I do and for my company. I am grateful for my God given gifts, talents, creativity and expertise. I open my self to share my gifts with others and make a difference to all that I work with.   I bless the money and abundance that comes to me through my work.   I am grateful for the clarity, focus and direction I have in my work and life.

BLESSING YOUR BOSS AND CO-WORKERS

Are you someone who enjoys spending time at work?

So many people spend so much time at work that their co-workers and boss actually become friends and sometimes feel as close as family.

Whether or not you like or get along with your boss and co-workers, it is beneficial for your well-being, productivity and spiritual growth to bless each person and wish the best for them. Blessing your boss and co-workers can really help to improve and uplift the energy where you work and create a more supportive, fun and productive environment.

I bless and give thanks for my boss, co-workers and all those that help me make my job so much easier. I am grateful for all that they do and the difference they make in my life. I am open and receptive to building better relationships with my co-workers and my boss. I am creating a work environment that I enjoy and excel in.

BLESSING YOUR SCHOOL AND TEACHERS

If you are in school or have children that are in school then this is an opportunity to bless and appreciate the institution of education. Our schools and teachers have a vital role in the wellbeing and future life of our children. One of my friend's daughters was having difficulty getting along with one of her high school teachers. She knew she had to change her attitude and decided that everyday she would bless her teacher and imagine her in a bubble of love. She found that after a short time her relationship with that teacher started to improve once she started blessing and feeling grateful for her.

I bless and appreciate my teachers and school. I am grateful for all that I have learned and thank God for my education and my ability to learn, grow and achieve all that I can. I bless all of my teachers who made such a difference in my life and were great role models.

BLESSING YOUR SPIRITUAL CENTER, CHURCH, SYNAGOGUE OR MOSQUE

Whether you belong to a spiritual center or not, it is good to bless and acknowledge all spiritual centers, churches, synagogues, sacred shrines, temples and mosques. Each of these are holy places and in their own way fulfills a divine mission and provides the community with spiritual support and comfort.

I give thanks and appreciate all spiritual centers and bless each and every church, temple, synagogue, shrine and mosque for the support that they provide to people and the community.

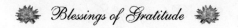

BLESSING FOR PEACE

As we see war and unrest happening around us, it is a reminder to stay focused on peace and a peaceful solution for all of us. As it has been said many times, if you seek peace in the world, you must first start with cultivating peace in your hearts and in your homes. We need to be that place of peace in the world.

Ask yourself, how can I bring more peace into my life this day and every day?

It is a good time to make peace with anyone that you are in conflict with and especially with yourself.

I bless the opportunity to be a role model for peace on this planet. I know that in order to do that, it must start within me first. I am willing to forgive myself and others for the hurtful and non-peaceful things that I have done and have been done to me. I am grateful for all I have and choose to create more peace and balance no matter what is happening in my life. I focus my thoughts and actions on a peaceful and harmonious solution. I am grateful for my life.

BLESSING THE GOVERNMENT

Have you ever felt that you wanted to do more to make this world a better place to live for all of us?

Blessing the government whether you agree with the powers that be or not gives you an opportunity to create a more positive and peaceful mind-set rather than one of anger and fear. We can make a difference by keeping ourselves clear and doing whatever we can.

Our government leaders, world leaders and those that are in power positions certainly can use all the blessings and prayers we can give to them. Our world needs our prayers and blessings to create a safe and peaceful place for all of us now and in the future.

God bless all of our world leaders. I offer my blessings and prayers of love and peace to our government and all those in power. I am grateful for this world and for all those with the vision and purpose to make our world a peaceful and safe place for all of us.

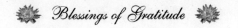

BLESSING YOUR PLANE FLIGHT

Does flying and traveling cause you to feel stressed?

Getting everything together for a trip and all that is required at the airport can certainly cause stress at times. Saying a blessing and being grateful for your flight and for the pilot and crew is a good way to release stress, relax your body and create more peace of mind.

I bless my flight, plane and all the crew. I thank God for this wonderful trip and know that I am surrounded by love and spiritually guided at all times. I am grateful for all I have, for feeling safe and for this wonderful new opportunity to relax and enjoy all that is around me. I bless my body and know it is full of energy and vitality.

BLESSING YOUR VACATION

Do you work really hard so that you can have a great vacation and then start your time off work feeling worried, stressed and tired?

This is a good opportunity to start your vacation from a relaxed and positive frame of mind. One of the ways to do this is by feeling grateful for your life and blessing this time of relaxation, rest and nurturing for your body, mind and soul. Before you go on your vacation, visualize in your mind everything going smoothly and having a wonderful and joyful time with your friends and loved ones.

I bless my vacation and know it is a time of rest, relaxation, renewal, adventure and fun. I am grateful for how easy everything flows and how much joy this trip brings to me and my family. I am uplifted, rested and I thank God for the gift of this vacation and for all the blessings in my life.

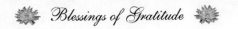

BLESSING YOUR COMMITMENTS AND DECISIONS

It can be challenging sometimes to keep our commitments or to make decisions for that matter, because by doing so it can bring up fears, doubt and concerns. We may all experience this at one time or another. Making commitments and decisions are a part of life and the more you can bless it, and see it as a blessing the easier it will be to feel confident in taking steps to move forward trusting what is right for you.

I bless every commitment and decision I make knowing that each one brings me to a higher level of growth, understanding and confidence in myself. I trust and know that the decisions I make are the right ones for me. I am grateful for the awareness that I can choose what direction and decision is suitable for me at every stage of my life. I am grateful to know that I am divinely guided in everything that I do.

BLESSINGS FOR SPECIAL OCCASIONS AND CEREMONIES

BLESSING FOR WEDDING CEREMONY

This is a sacred and holy ceremony bringing two lives and two hearts together as one.
It is a commitment of unconditional love and willingness to be there to support and uplift one another. The commitment you are making is one to bring out the best in each other and to live your divine purpose as individuals and as a couple.

I bless our divine marriage, our commitment and our life together, knowing it is one brought forth through God's love and grace. I am grateful for the love that we share and this amazing journey we are choosing to take together. I know that our only competition is to see who can love the most and who can forgive the fastest. I give great thanks for the gift of my beloved in my life.

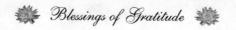

Irish Wedding Blessing

"May the road rise to meet you.   May the wind be always at your back.   May the sun shine warm upon your face, the rains fall soft upon the fields.

May the light of friendship guide your paths together. May the laughter of children grace the halls of your home. May the joy of living for one another trip a smile from your lips, a twinkle from your eye.   And when eternity beckons, at the end of a life heaped high with love, may the good Lord embrace you with the arms that have nurtured you the whole length of your joy-filled days. May the gracious God hold you both in the palm of His Hands.   And, today, may the Spirit of Love find a dwelling place in your hearts."

(Author unknown)

BLESSING FOR BIRTH

Irish Proverb: *"What the child sees, the child does, what the child does, the child is."*

Bringing a new life into this world is surely a sacred and joyous celebration. It is a time to give thanks for all the blessings and to welcome in this beautiful and divine spirit and child of God into your life and family.

I bless and give thanks for the miracle of this birth and new life. I know that the process of birth is divinely guided and I have all the love and support I need. I bless my child and thank God for him/her.

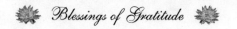
BABY NAMING AND BABY BLESSING

This is a wonderful opportunity to spiritually welcome this child into his/her family, community and into the world. It is a time to bless and recognize this divine being and child of God and to recognize his/her family. It is a special opportunity to let this child know that he/she is loved and appreciated for the loving presence that they are and to celebrate the sacredness of their name and spirit.

May this child of God be blessed with a life full of joy, love and laughter. I bless this child and know that he/she lives their soul's purpose and makes a difference to all who he/she meets. I pray that this child always remembers the spiritual truth about who he/she is and shares his/her love and joy with others. I bless this child's name and know that it is sacred and holy as it represents who he/she is.

BLESSING FOR COMING OF AGE

Coming of age and initiation ceremonies signify the passage from childhood to adulthood. This is a very sacred time that needs to be celebrated and acknowledged. In Judaism, coming of age is signified by a spiritual celebration known as Bar and Bat Mitzvah. This literally means "son or daughter of the commandment" and signifies the time when a child becomes responsible for observing and following the commandments and rules of Jewish life. In other cultures coming of age for girls is marked by her first menstruation. It can also be marked by receiving a tattoo or having one's ear pierced. Some of the Native American tribes have a period of isolation for their children coming of age, where the women gather together and the men do a vision quest.

I bless and am grateful for this wonderful "coming of age" from childhood to adulthood. I know that it is a sacred and empowering time and I have all the love and support I need. I move forward becoming more of who I am with clarity, direction and love. I am grateful for this time of growth, change, friendship and initiation. I am open to receive the divine grace of God in my life.

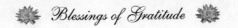
BLESSING FOR BIRTHDAYS

Did you know that the day you were born is a sacred day and one to be acknowledged and celebrated?

Your birthday is a special time to reflect on all the people who you have loved and who have loved you and whose life is better because you were in it. Spend time on this day in gratitude and thanksgiving for all you have in your life and for all the blessings. Do something today that you love and enjoy and celebrate you and the difference you make to all who know you.

I bless and am grateful to God for this day of my birth and celebrate my life and all the love and grace that I have experienced. I celebrate my birthday and am grateful for all the blessings in my life. I choose to express joy, appreciation and love from my heart today.

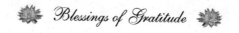
BLESSING FOR GRADUATION

Graduation marks a time of achievement, celebration and new beginnings. In a way, it is like a rite of passage from where you were to where you are now going. Take this time to acknowledge yourself and loved ones who are graduating. This is a time of awakening to new possibilities and opportunities. Celebrate every step of this great journey, called life.

I bless this time of graduation knowing that it is a new beginning for my life. I am proud of myself for my accomplishments and stand in my confidence and faith that all is in perfect order in my life. I thank God for all the blessings and for this time of growth and discovering more about my purpose and doing what I love and am good at.

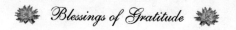

BLESSING FOR RETIREMENT

The perceptions and beliefs that you have around this stage of life can make all the difference. This is an opportunity to let go of fear, experience new things and do what you have always wanted to do. It is never too late to start now and step out of what is comfortable and try something new. Every moment counts so discover what makes you happy and live your life to the fullest.

I bless this time of change and letting go of what I know and have been used to. I am grateful for all the new opportunities opening up to me. I am ready to experience my life with fulfillment, love and excitement. I bless and thank God for this new adventure that I am embarking upon.

BLESSING FOR THE FULL MOON

Have you ever felt emotions rise and experienced being more sensitive than usual when the moon is full?

This is a time of great power and change for all and especially for women. Women's menstrual cycles are said to be connected to the moon.

The full moon and changes in the moon are celebrated as rituals and spiritual gathering for fulfilling our prayers, wishes, projects and life events. It is a time for clarity, creativity and for blessing all that you have in your life.

I bless this sacred time of the full moon and thank God for the beauty and abundant healing power that is the moon and mother nature. I call forth and open myself to all that I need to know to express my creativity, love and joy fully. I give great thanks for the opening and expansion of my heart, body, spirit and mind.

BLESSINGS FOR MAJOR HOLIDAYS
～◦～

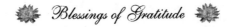

NEW YEAR

This is a time to begin anew, to look ahead and plan for the future. It is a time to settle old debts and set goals for the New Year. In many cultures it is celebrated with a thorough housecleaning and a sweeping out of the old. New Year's Eve can be a night of celebration in many cultures as young and old alike stay up to welcome in the New Year, often with loud noisemakers, singing and toasting to good cheer. Others welcome in the New Year in a quiet and meditative way with loved ones.

I bless and welcome in the New Year with an open heart and an open mind. I release all that I do not need from the past year and know that each day is a new beginning. I thank God for the opportunity to experience new things this year and to bring more love and joy into my life. I call forth a year of abundance, good health, love, joy, peace and blessings for myself and for others.

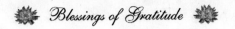

CHINESE NEW YEAR

Celebrated in January and lasts approximately one week with festivities, fireworks, colored lights, lanterns, parades, special meals with family and is a time of giving gifts and celebrating. It is one of the biggest holidays in the Chinese culture.

I give great thanks and bless this celebration of the New Year and of the spring to come. I am grateful for my ancestors and for all the blessings in my life and thank God for my family and friends.

PASSOVER - CELEBRATING FREEDOM

Passover is a celebration and signifies the passage from slavery to freedom. Since the bread the Jews baked for their flight was unleavened, on Passover all flour products are removed from the home and only unleavened bread (known as matzot) is eaten. The ritual Seder dinner includes a ceremonial plate containing a roasted shank bone (symbolizing the sacrificed lamb), a roasted egg (symbol of fertility and renewal), bitter herbs, usually horseradish (symbol of bitter times of slavery), greens such as parsley (representing spring and renewal), kharoset, which can be made up of chopped apples, fruit, cinnamon, wine and ground nuts (symbolizing the mortar used by the enslaved Jews), a cup of salt water which signifies the tears of the Israelites and three matzot (unleavened bread) representing the three tribes of Israel, Kohanim, Levites and Israelites.

I am grateful to God for all the blessings that are in my life. I give great thanks for this time of celebration, freedom, being with family and friends. This is a blessing of love and freedom for all human beings no matter their race, color or religion. I give thanks for all who came before me to create more freedom and blessings for us all.

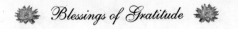

EASTER

Easter first began as a Pagan festival of welcoming and celebrating the season of spring.

In the Christian faith, Easter is a holy week celebrating and commemorating the life and resurrection of Jesus Christ. The Lenten season leading up to Easter Sunday for many is a time of fasting, inner reflection and prayer. Every country and individual celebrates this sacred and holy time in their special way.

I bless this time of rebirth and holy sacrament. I am grateful for this sacred time of renewal. I bless my family and my spirituality. I am grateful to God for my life and all the blessings I have. I give thanks for beauty of the earth and all the seasons.

ROSH HASHANAH – JEWISH NEW YEAR

This holiday begins a ten-day period also known as the ten days of repentance and continues through Yom Kippur. This is a time when Jewish families and friends come together for services, prayers and to share food. They join together to celebrate the New Year and all the blessings and goodness in their lives as well as asking for forgiveness for their shortcomings.

I am grateful to God for another year of love, peace, family and health. I bless my family and all who I love and care about. I thank God for the blessings that fill my life each day. I bless this Jewish New Year and call forth that each and every day be made anew.

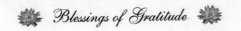

Yom Kippur – Day Of Atonement

Yom Kippur is marked by a twenty-four hour fast and prayers asking God for forgiveness for all the transgressions during the year. This is a heartfelt time of experiencing deeper compassion, tolerance and love for ourselves and others. On the eve of Yom Kippur and on the following day, the Jewish community gathers together in the synagogue for prayer and reflection. Friends and families join after sunset on the first day to break the fast with delicious food, drink and celebration.

I bless this holy time and forgive myself and others. I give thanks for my family, my life and my health. I am grateful for this time of prayer and reflection. I open my heart to experience greater love and compassion for all people.

RAMADAN

Ramadan is the ninth month of the Islamic Calendar.   It is a time of giving charity, getting closer to God through prayer and fasting. Muslim people fast from sunrise to sunset.   It is the month of the Qur'an, the month of mercy, the month of forgiveness, the month of prayer at night and Suhoor, the month of solidarity and mutual help, the month of all blessings.

I give thanks to Allah for my life and all of its beauty and holiness.   I am grateful for the love in my heart and for this time of closeness to God through devotion, good deeds and purifying my body.   I call forth and hold the vision of peace on this planet for all mankind.

THANKSGIVING

In the United States, this holiday is a time to gather around the table and share a blessed meal with your loved ones and to thank God for all that you have. It is a time to celebrate the gifts of the harvest and express gratitude with family and friends. Wherever you may live, take the time each day to express your love and gratitude for your family and the people you are close to that make a difference in your life.

I give thanks and appreciation for all that I have and for all the blessings in my life. I am grateful to God for this meal we are about to eat and for this time of sharing with family and loved ones. I am grateful for all the miracles and for each joyous moment of life. Thank you God for all the love I have in my life.

CHANUKAH – CELEBRATION OF LIGHTS

This is a joyous and festive time when families gather each night to light the menorah (candelabra) and say a prayer of gratitude for all the blessings and to remember the victory of the Maccabees and the miraculous amount of oil that burned for eight days. In some families, a gift is exchanged after the candles are lit.

I give thanks for God, Divine Spirit, Source of Life, who makes us holy through his commandments and prayers. I am grateful to God for and our ancestors for all the miracles during this time and throughout the year. Blessed are you God for life itself.

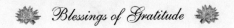

CHRISTMAS — CELEBRATING THE CHRIST PRESENCE

Christmas is a time of commemorating the birth of Jesus of Nazareth. Christmas celebrations range from a quiet religious observance to the rowdy carnivals as seen in many of the Caribbean Islands. It is a time for family members to appreciate each other and enjoy this festive time. Friends and families celebrate with presents and loved ones coming together to share food, blessings and prayer.

I bless and celebrate the Christ Presence in my life. I rejoice and am so grateful for this sacred time of year, for the love of family, friends and for the grace and love of God.

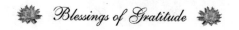

KWANZAA

This is an African Harvest Festival celebrated on December 26. It was started by Dr. Maulana Karenga and it celebrates the fruits of the harvest. On each of the seven nights, a candle is lit in special seven-branched candelabra, representing the seven principles of African Society. They are: unity, self-determination, collective work and responsibility, cooperative economics, purpose, creativity and faith.

I am grateful and thankful for the grace of God in my life. I celebrate the fruits of the harvest and all the bounty and abundance that are all around this sacred earth. I am grateful for my faith, for all that I have and for my loved ones.

SPIRITUAL AND CULTURAL BLESSINGS

SPIRITUAL AND CULTURAL BLESSINGS

Because this blessing book is all about honoring all people, cultures and religions, the following are special blessings and prayers from many different cultures around the world. A majority of these cultural blessings have come from a prayer site on the internet. They did not include the author of these blessings and prayers. It was important to me to include a variety of cultural blessings as we are all children of God. There are many more beautiful cultural blessings and prayers that have not been included here and I hope you enjoy the ones that I have chosen. My vision and dream is that one day we can all live together on this beautiful planet in gratitude, peace, respect and harmony.

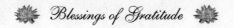

JEWISH BLESSING
THE SHEMA

This sacred blessing simply declares that God is one.   Many people recite the "Shema" once in the morning and once in the evening. Growing up Jewish, this blessing has always made me feel ever more connected to God.

Sh'ma Yisra'el Adonai Eloheinu Adonai Echad

English Translation: "Hear, O Israel, the Lord our God, the Lord is one."

JEWISH BLESSING
THE SHECHECHIANU

This blessing is recited for almost any special occasion such as Bar and Bat Mitzvah, important milestones and holidays such as Rosh Hashanah.   This is a blessing that awakens us to the splendor and sacredness of each moment.

Barukh Atah Adonai, Eloheinu Melekh Ha-olam,

Shehekheyanu, V'kiyimanu, V'higiyanu Laz'man Hazeh

English translation: "Blessed are you, Lord our God, Ruler of the Universe, who has given us life, sustained us and allowed us to reach this day."

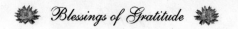

ISLAMIC BEDTIME BLESSING

"In Thy name, Lord, I lay me down and
In Thy name will I rise up.
O God, Thou art the first and before Thee there is nothing;
Thou art the last and after Thee there is nothing;
Thou art the outmost and above Thee there is nothing;
Thou art the inmost and below Thee there is nothing.
Waken me, O God, in the hour most pleasing to Thee
and use me in the works most pleasing to Thee,
that Thou mayest bring me ever nearer to Thyself."

Sanskrit Salutation To The Dawn

"Listen to the salutation to the dawn, look to this day for it is life, the very life of life.   In its brief course lie all the verities and realities of our existence, the bliss of growth, the splendor of beauty.   For yesterday is but a dream and tomorrow is only a vision, today well spent makes every yesterday a dream of happiness and every tomorrow a vision of hope.   Look well therefore to this day, such is the salutation to the dawn."

TRADITIONAL BUDDHIST BLESSING AND HEALING CHANT

"Just as the soft rains fill the streams,
pour into the rivers and join together in the oceans,
so may the power of every moment of your goodness
flow forth to awaken and heal all beings;
those here now, those gone before, those yet to come.

By the power of every moment of your goodness,
may your heart's wishes be soon fulfilled
as completely shining as the bright full moon,
as magically as by a wish-fulfilling gem.

By the power of every moment of your goodness,
may all dangers be averted and all disease be gone.
May no obstacle come across your way.
May you enjoy fulfillment and long life.

For all in whose heart dwells respect,
who follow the wisdom and compassion, of the way;
may your life prosper in the four blessings
of old age, beauty, happiness and strength."

Sikh Prayer For Abundance

"May the kingdom of justice prevail!
May the believers be united in love!
May the hearts of the believers be humble, high their
wisdom.
May they be guided in their wisdom by the Lord.
Glory be to God!
Entrust unto the Lord what thou wishes to be
accomplished.
The Lord will bring all matters to fulfillment.
Know this as truth evidenced by Himself."

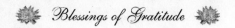

CHRISTIAN BLESSING FROM THE INDIAN ORTHODOX CHURCH

"Grant us Lord, God, that while our bodies rest from the labors of the day and as our souls are released from the thoughts of this world, we may stand in Thy presence with tranquility and quietness in this evening hour.

Make us worthy to offer Thee ceaseless praise and thanksgiving without interruption.

May we acknowledge Thy loving kindness and mercy by which Thou dost rule and direct. Unto Thee we offer praise and thanksgiving now and unto ages of ages, Amen."

A CATHOLIC BLESSING FOR THE HOME

"Bless our home, Father and all who live here in peace. May we all love you and know the love you have for us."

WELSH BLESSING

"Grant us, O God, your protection; and in your protection, strength; and in strength, understanding; and in understanding, knowledge; and in knowledge, the knowledge of justice; and in the knowledge of justice, the love of justice; and in that love, the love of existence; and in the love of existence, the love of God, God and all goodness, Amen."

GUARDIAN ANGEL BLESSING

"Guardian Angel from heaven so bright,
watching beside me to lead me aright.
Fold thy wings round me, and guard me with love,
Softly sing songs to me of heaven above."

CLOSING MESSAGE

I bless you on this sacred journey of your life. We are all connected and it is by blessings and prayers that we can continue to stay in touch with our heart, soul and God. This book is all about bringing us back to a place of gratitude, which is one of the highest spiritual principles we can live by. The more we can see the events that occur in our life as a blessing, the greater joy, love and spiritual oneness we are able to feel and experience.

The blessings in this book have made a real difference to my life. I hope you enjoy the blessings in this book and that they have added great value and have given you a deeper sense of peace, love and beauty in your life. I encourage you to be open to say whatever blessing you choose and see for yourself what happens.

I would love to hear all the ways that the blessings in this book have helped and inspired your life. Please let me know which blessings you would like to see added to the next Blessings Of Gratitude Book.

May the blessings of God surround and uplift you. May God's light shine bright and grant you a long life of good health, love, joy and peace. May peace prevail for all people.

Namaste,
Laurie Leah Levine

Laurie Leah Levine is a gifted international healer and the spiritual director and founder of Positive Living Spiritual Centre in Sydney, Australia. It is non-denominational and based on principles of spirituality and science of mind. The purpose of the centre is to enrich people's lives through love, acceptance and spirituality. Laurie is a Metaphysical Minister, Master Practitioner of Neuro Linguistic Programing and Developer of Emotional Release Point Therapy. She has a background in acupressure, energetic healing, metaphysics, spiritual counseling, emotional release, cranial sacral therapy and nursing.

Laurie has a holistic health practice and offers healing sessions by telephone and in person, relationship classes, healing and spirituality workshops and talks.

The following are some of the topics Laurie covers:
- Creating Intimate Relationships
- Living A Spiritual Life - The Healing Power Of Blessings & Gratitude
- Body Rapport & Healing From The Inside Out
- Are You Addicted To Stress?
  Practical Tools For Preventing Adrenal Burnout

Other Services Laurie Offers Include:
- Spiritual Development & Healing Programs
- Relationship Classes with her husband Stan
- Women's Retreats
- Sacred Ceremonies, Rituals and Spiritual Services
- Keynote Presentations and Conference Break-out Sessions
- Corporate Wellness Coaching and Consulting

Contact Laurie for more information on her healing and coaching sessions, spiritual center activities and other services offered. Have her speak at your conference or add value to your organization. Laurie is available for radio and television interviews.

To order your copy of her International *Spiritual Medicine* book, her healing meditation and relaxation CD's as well as *Blessings of Gratitude* book, see Laurie's website: www.laurielevine.com. You can email Laurie at: laurieleahlevine@hotmail.com or laurielevine@optusnet.com.au

References

Blessings For Special Occasions And Ceremonies

Blessings for coming of age – *Bar and Bat Mitzvah* by Bert Metter – Clarion Books, 1984, Pages 7-8.

(Authors of the internet blessings were not listed)

Irish Wedding Blessing: http://www.1stholistic.com/ Spl_prayers

Spiritual and Cultural Blessings

Jewish Blessing– The Shema:
http://www.jewfaq.org/prayer/shema.htm

Shechechianu Blessing – *Essential Judaism* by George Robinson. Pocket Books, 2000, Page 93.

Islamic through Welsh Blessing:
http://www.1stholistic.com/Spl_prayers

Catholic Blessing – Catholic Doors Ministry 2003
http://www.catholicdoors.com/payer/english/p01096.htm

Guardian Angel Blessing
http://www.webdesk.com/catholic/prayers/

Holiday Blessings

Chinese New Year:
http://www.holidayinsights.com/other/cnewyr.htm

Passover - Information from: *Essential Judaism* by
George Robinson. Pocket Books, 2000, Pages121 - 123.

Easter – http://www.holidayinsights.com/easter/

Rosh Hashanah - *Essential Judaism* by George Robinson.
Pocket Books 2000, Page 93.Other references came from:
http://www.jewfaq.org/prayer/roshhash.htm

Yom Kippur - *Essential Judaism* by George Robinson.
Pocket Books, 2000, Pages 97-100.

Ramadan: http://www.omanaccess.com/accessramadhan/
ramadanprayers.asp and http://www.islam.australia.com.au

Chanukah Blessing: http://www.ritualwell.org

Kwanzaa: *http*://www.officialkwanzaawebsite.org